Seeds
of
Destiny

A Faith Filled Journey to
Fulfilling Your Dreams

CARY PALMON

For Information Contact:
Cary Palmon Ministries
P.O. Box 54723
Tulsa, OK 74155
Email: cpm@carypalmon.org

Printed in the USA

Table of Contents

Dedication

It is with great pleasure that I dedicate this book to the
many friends and partners of this ministry
who have faithfully prayed with me, who have contributed
generous financial support, and who have believed together
with me for the seemingly impossible dream of reaching
vast numbers of the lost for Christ.

God has accomplished much
through the "grain of mustard seed" I've planted,
thanks to many people just like you.
I hold you dear in my heart and in my prayers.

I also want to express my gratitude to
Dr. Jess Bair for the revision of the manuscript and
to Wenzel Design for all the artwork and graphic design
that they provided to this ministry, including this book.

And last but not least, I want to dedicate this book to my family
and thank them for standing by my side and believing
in my dream. Through the years they would tease me, saying,
"Go Cary Kuhlman," or "What is Mother Theresa doing now?"
They have never doubted that I had a true calling and purpose
to bring the Gospel to the lost. I have been blessed
with a wonderful family!

Introduction

Many of God's children have dreams that have not yet come to pass, and they wonder if the dream will ever become a reality. I remember when I was such a person. For years I dreamed about reaching multitudes of people for Christ, because when I met Jesus Christ as my Savior, He made such an impact on my life that I wanted everyone to experience the same love, the same healing power, and the same restoration that I received.

Today that dream is no longer merely a dream; it is now a reality. You are about to read how God established it. Maybe it is different from the most common ways of establishing a ministry, but it is the way God has led me, and the results have been overwhelming, first to me, and then to others who hear about it. God is the Creator, and many people think that He only moves within certain parameters, but that is a mental block to the greatness of God and our personal faith. We must take the limits off if we want to reach our destiny. God has no limits, so why should we limit Him?

I want to tell you how my journey started so that it will give you the faith and courage to go forward and eventually see your dreams come to pass. God is not a respecter of persons; what He does for one of his children, He will certainly do for another. What He did for me, He'll do for you. As you read how He led me, believe that He has a special way in which He wants to lead you to fulfill your dream. So, open your heart, reach out in faith to complete your vision, and let your dreams become a reality as well.

7

CHAPTER 1

A SEED IS PLANTED

The story you are about to read might seem incredible to some of you. However, all the facts in it are real. It is a story of intrigue, treason, murder, and miracles. It is a story of how God can take broken lives, restore them, and make good of all the bad that happened in those lives.

It was a beautiful fall morning several years ago, the leaves had started to change colors, and in

Oklahoma it is a very delightful time.
The weather was just perfect, and one could
easily get caught up in looking at the beauty
of the landscape. It was during those days that
I had been invited by an acquaintance named
MaryAnn to attend a ladies' prayer meeting.
MaryAnn was very insistent, and she would not
take "no" for an answer. I remember well when
I walked into the church for the first time, all
frightened and very uncomfortable because I
had never been to such meetings, and I was not
sure what I was going to find. I had asked my
mother to take care of my children, who at that
time were very young. Even though I really
did not want to attend the meeting, I could not
dodge Mary Ann's persistent wheedling anymore.

When I arrived at the church, I chose to sit at the
end of the aisle so I could make a quick escape. I
looked around to see what was going on, and I
realized that there was a small group of women
in a very serene state of worship, and they were

singing a simple song whose only word was "Alleluia." I am sure that you have heard it, but it was new to my ears at that time. In the midst of that song I sensed the presence of God for the first time in my life, and I heard Him saying to me, "Cary, you have not loved me, you have not let me be number one in your life!" My heart was broken, tears started to come out of my heart; I knew this was God, and He was right. I had been selfish. I never had time for Him, and I had not honored Him during my life. The awareness of my own selfish life was stronger by the minute, and with it there was a great anguish in my heart. I was weeping softly, and I bent down to pick up a Kleenex from my purse when my eyes fell on the Bible that Mary Ann had in her lap.

A Bible verse jumped out at me. I read it, and it said, "Accept me as your Lord and Savior and you and your house will be saved." As I read those words, I turned my heart to God and said, "Lord, I accept you as my Lord and Savior."

When I said that, the anguish that was in my heart stopped, and instead I was filled with great joy. The tears were still coming out, but these were tears of joy!

I sat through the meeting, and I remember feeling God's love being poured out to me, enveloping me in forgiveness, in love, and in acceptance. There was wave after wave of love being poured into me. I knew God loved me, and He was real!

After the meeting, the ladies gathered in a circle to testify what God had done for them. Suddenly someone pushed me, and I found myself in the center of a circle with lots of eyes looking at me. One of the ladies asked, "What happened to you?" and all I could respond was, " I know God!" All the women were so happy, and I wondered why. You see, I had never heard the Gospel, so I did not know I could be saved. I did know that I was lost, but I did not know how I could escape the fate that would wait for me the day I died. I had never read a Bible or attended any type of service where the Gospel was being proclaimed. I was raised Catholic, but my attendance in Catholic churches was limited to a couple of times a year, just to make my conscience feel a bit better. However, deep inside of me, I knew that some day a terrible fate was waiting for me.

At the end of the gathering, the women started to pick up their Bibles and were chatting with each other. A lady, who was a little older than I was, came to me and asked if I wanted to receive the Baptism of the Holy Spirit. I looked her right in the eye and asked her what I thought to be the most important question possible at that exact moment. It was: "Will I feel happier than what I am now?" She smiled and said, "Honey, you will." And with that, I gave my hand to this little stranger, and she led me to the front of the room to visit with the speaker for that morning study. She told me

to ask Jesus to fill me with His Holy Spirit.
I thought her to be quite an educated lady
because I noticed that while she talked to the
audience, she would talk in Latin as well. I
would later learn that instead of Latin, she was
speaking in tongues!

She told me to ask to be filled with the Holy Spirt,
and I did. Then I decided to take advantage
of the situation and talk to the Lord in Spanish
so these ladies would not know what I was
saying--mainly because I felt a little embarrassed
that they would hear me. I started in Spanish
to form the words "Te quiero," which means, "I
love you," but suddenly something happened to
me. Out of my own throat these strange sounds
came out, and they sounded like words. My
thoughts went wild, and part of me was saying,
"Stop it! You are crazy! Stop these sounds.
What is going on?" But my heart was saying,
"Go, girl! Go." The more I talked, the happier
my heart would feel. The logical side of my

being would fight this new experience, and for a little while there was a genuine battle going on inside me, but it did not take long for my heart to win. I felt like I was talking to God, and He was talking back to me. It was so wonderful!

A few minutes later, I felt a small push in my back and I realized that the ladies were closing the church building and leaving, and there I stood, at the door of the church, speaking in some kind of language that I have never heard, happy as I had never been before, crying, singing, without my usual self control, and waving goodbye at all the ladies as they left the church parking lot.

Well, what do you do when the Holy Ghost gets ahold of you? I went to my car, I started driving around the city, and I continued speaking in this wonderful language. I sang, I cried, and I sang some more. I told God I loved Him. He told me He loved me, and the time went on. After a while--and to this date I really don't recall how

long I was driving around, but I presume it was
a couple of hours, I felt that whatever got ahold
of me was subsiding, and I could speak in both
English and Spanish again. So I went home
to my mother, who was watching my children,
and she was really worried about me since I had
been gone for a fairly long time. When I arrived,
she saw an evident change in me.

Immediately she inquired what had happened
to me, and I related the series of events that had
transpired earlier in the evening. I told her that
now God was so real to me, and I knew that He
loved me. Mother wanted to know God this way
as well, and she asked me to call MaryAnn to come
and tell us what took place. I called her, and she
said she would come to our house that evening.

I was so captured with the joy of knowing God
that I called my relatives, and they were all at the
house waiting for the lady to show up and tell
us what was going on and why was I speaking in

some kind of strange language. You know, the gift of tongues is a great sign to the unbeliever!!!!

So, the evening arrived, and all of us were in great expectation of what MaryAnn was going to say. She came with her Bible and explained to all us of that I had been born again and that I was filled with the Holy Spirit with the evidence of speaking in tongues. At the end of the evening, my whole family accepted the Lord as their Savior and they were filled with the Holy Spirit. The promise of the Lord that my family would be saved was fulfilled that same day!

I remember the joy that was in my heart during those days, and I remember my hunger to know Him and to read the Bible so I would learn who He is and what would make Him happy and what would not. I knew that He had come into my life to mend all my broken pieces, and I needed it because I was badly broken on the inside!

The reason I was so terribly broken was because of my past. I was born in Cuba, and during Castro's takeover of my country my father was brutally executed while fighting for the religious and political freedom of Cuba. The man that turned him in was my dad's protégé, and he came to our house to identify my dad. When the police took my father, the rest of the family became prisoners in our own home, and we watched them tear everything apart, looking for incriminating evidence against my father. I think they stayed at our house for a couple of days searching and arresting anyone that came to visit. My mother, my little sister, and I hung together with great fear. In the meantime, they took my father to a terrible prison in Havana that was an old run-down Spanish castle called La Cabaña. He was incarcerated there for about three months.

I kept asking my mother when my daddy would return home, and she said it would be soon.

One day she was very agitated, and she asked me to take care of my sister and make sure that we both went to bed at the regular time. She told me she would be very late that evening. So my sister and I went to bed, as we did every night, not aware that on that night my daddy was being tried and immediately sentenced to death at the age of 37. That same evening, at one a.m., they walked him to the execution wall and shot him to death.

Around five a.m. my aunt came to the house and woke me up. She said for me to get ready. I had no idea what was going on. I was 15 years old and had been raised in the traditional Cuban notion that a young person would never question her elders. So I got dressed and followed my aunt. As we were going down the stairs, she turned around and told me that my dad had been executed and that my mother needed me in the awaiting taxi.

I had heard my aunt's words, but I could not receive them. I keep telling myself that this was only a nightmare. But then I saw my mother cry and scream, "Murderers! Please, kill me too!" I realized that what my aunt had said was true. My father had been executed, and the horrible truth sank into my heart. I had not known that my father was involved in fighting for the freedom of the country. There were so many questions in my heart, but no one would talk about it, for there was great fear in all of our hearts.

My mother was not able to handle the horrible tragedy, and on the same day of his death she started taking sleeping pills to cope with her loss. I was suddenly left alone to take care of my seven-year-old sister. The night of my father's death I vowed that I would never forgive the man that turned him in to Castro's secret police, nor would I forgive anyone else involved in his violent death. It was the darkest night of my life, and a root of hate and bitterness came into my life along with a very broken heart. That night I was changed, and it was indeed a very sad change!

Those times were very dangerous in Cuba. We were marked as potential "traitors" to the new regime. Since my dad had been executed, everyone knew we did not approve of Castro's communist dictatorship. My family decided to leave the country. Any young person was in great danger, because every day that passed, Castro was implementing laws to get a hold of the young people and brainwash them. Due to my age, I certainly would eventually wind up among those to be brainwashed. But before it could happen, my mother made the decision to depart from Cuba, and we applied for a visa to leave the country. The Cuban Immigration Department came and took a complete inventory of our possessions. They said that if anything was missing from the home, our visa would be cancelled. Thus, when the day arrived to leave for the United States, we were only allowed a suitcase of clothing and pictures of our loved ones.

We landed in Miami, Florida, just like the majority of refugees that were leaving Cuba. Some were able to escape with all their families; others were children that were sent to the Catholic Charities programs, and others were young people that family members, who had already emigrated, would receive. We were a most pitiful group. We all had a common bond of broken hearts, broken dreams, and broken families.

A friend of my father was very gracious to us and rented us a tiny garage apartment. We had nothing--no money and no job. But we were not alone, since so many other Cubans were in the same condition. I was fortunate to speak some English, and I fairly quickly found employment in a hardware store running the cash register. At that time my earnings were around 65 cents per hour. I had just turned 16, and I had become the breadwinner of the house. My little sister started elementary school, and my mother continued taking sleeping pills to deal with the loss of my dad. These were the unhappiest times of my young life. I would cry at night for my dad, and I would hate the man that caused this terrible tragedy in our lives. I created mental lists of all the reasons why I hated him, and it would be like this: "You killed my father. Because of you I lost my language, my culture, my future, my home, my dreams!" In my pain and anguish I would feed the terrible hatred that I had in my heart towards that man and the communist regime.

We lived in Florida for a couple of years, and for some reason that I still do not fully understand, we ended up in Tulsa, Oklahoma. It was a good thing, because by that time my mother had started to mend, and she went to work. Little by little, she was able to incorporate herself back into society. My sister continued to go to school, and I found employment in our new city. Through the years I would ask my mother the details concerning my father's accusation and his death, but she would start crying, and I would not proceed because of the great pain she would experience. It took me years to find out more about it, and it was only recently that I found out about his work and the situations that brought him to an early death. I also found out that he belonged to a very strong Catholic organization that was opposed to the lack of freedom of religion imposed by the Castro regime.

When Daddy died, I did not see his body, but my mother did, and she said he had a smile on his face. Over and over I would say to myself, "Dad, how could you have had a smile when you are leaving us behind?" That answer came recently while I was visiting my cousin Vivian in Miami, and she asked me if I knew what had transpired during my father's last hours. I replied, "You know that Mother will not talk about it, so I have no idea of what happened" and then I asked her, "How could you know if he was behind bars?" She proceeded to tell me that within that place, all the prisoners could hear what was going on at the execution grounds and word came back to my family informing them of his last hours on this earth. He also left a letter, that I treasure greatly, telling each one of us how much he loved us and that he was looking forward to seeing us again. My cousin told me that my father and fourteen other men were accused of underground guerrilla work. During the trial my father declared himself the only guilty one, thus saving the lives of the other fourteen men that were probably going to be executed along with him. That very night, right after he was pronounced guilty, they walked him to the execution wall. They asked him if he wanted to be blindfolded and he declined. His last words were "All Hail King Jesus"! For years I had questioned many times if he had an encounter with God. Now I know he did, and my walk with Christ is the result of his prayers for me.

We had lived in Tulsa, Oklahoma, for about two years when I met a young man, and we got married. We had children, and I was very happy being a mother. I felt I had a home again. But my husband had other plans, and one day he announced that he wanted a divorce because his desires were totally different than mine. He wanted to be involved in parties, girls, drugs, and alcohol. A wife and kids were not part of his plans, so he left us. Again, my old friends, hate and bitterness came out every night to remind me how much I hated him right along with the men involved in my father's death.

Time went on, and it was about one year after he left us that I went to the prayer meeting where I met Jesus. I had been really broken inside. My life was a mess. I was working non-stop to support my children, and worse yet, my heart was full of hate. After the glorious experience that I had with the Lord, I would hear Him saying, "Cary let's talk about the man that turned your dad in." I would respond, "Ask me whatever you want, but don't ask me to forgive him."

And He would let me be.

Time would roll around, and again I would hear Him repeating the same question. As before, He would get the same answer. However, the day came when His love compelled me to change the answer, and I said, "OK, let's talk about him and all the other people that I hate." His Grace came in. I was able to forgive. I prayed for my enemies. I chose to forget the wrong done to us. As I set my enemies free from my hatred, I also was set free!

Sometimes I reflect on the wonderful work that God does in the heart of a person, and I realize He does all things well. He exceeds all our expectations! I would never imagine that I would be healed from the horrible experience of my father's death.

Two years passed, and I was sitting at a Bible seminar when a young lady came towards me. She said, "The Lord has a Word for you." It was Isaiah 60:4 –

> *Lift up your eyes round about you and see!*
> *They all gather themselves together, they come*
> *to you. Your sons shall come from afar, and your*
> *daughters shall be carried and nursed in the arms*
> > *(Amplified Bible)*

Wow! I was to have sons and daughters from all the parts of the earth! How would God do that? I prayed that God would let it be unto me according to His Word.

A seed was planted....

CHAPTER 2

UNLESS THE SEED FALLS TO THE GROUND...

More years went by. One day I heard God whisper
in my ear, "I am going to send you to the Latin
American people" I thought to myself, "Oh no,
I don't have a Spanish Bible! I don't know how
to sing Spanish Christian songs! Are you sure?"
But soon after that I found myself pioneering
the first Spirit-filled Hispanic church in Tulsa.
I loved being a pastor! I have asked myself many
times, how did it start?

I ran into some old friends from my pre-Christ-
centered days, and they were broken hearted
either because of their own physical problems
or because of problems that their children were
having. I invited them to come to my house
to offer prayer in their behalf, and guess what!
They were healed. They gave their hearts to Jesus.
Their children came to the Lord. They told
their friends. They brought their friends. Their
friends received Christ. They were healed. Their
homes were restored. They told their friends,
and so on. Jesus was doing in my home the
same things He did in the Bible--saving, healing,
loving, restoring, and before long He gave us a
wonderful location where we could hold services
on a regular basis. And so, He made me a
pastor with many sheep from many different
countries of Latin America. During this period
I remembered the word of prophecy that had
been given to me earlier when I was told that He
would bring me children from many nations. I
thought, "This is it!" I was very happy seeing so

many people's lives changed and so many answers to prayers, but I was thinking too small.

During the time that I was serving as a pastor I knew that the city would eventually have many more Hispanic residents, and I started to pray that we would have a Spanish church in every neighborhood. Twenty years later, this city is full of Spanish churches—both large and small. God has allowed me to see the answer to my prayers.

While I was pastoring, God started to lay on my heart the burden to see my native country saved. Cuba was going through terrible times; the government was being really hard on the Church. I would cry for the lost souls in my native land. I would weep for their lack of material needs as well as for their need for God, for all the blood of the martyrs that was being spilled, for the many widows and orphans that were broken hearted as my family and I were once upon a time. And while in prayer I sensed a shift in my heart toward evangelism. I was no longer satisfied with the local church. I wanted to find these lost people and tell them that Jesus could mend their hearts and lives just like He did for me.

Before long, I was drawn to go to Miami, home of a very large number of Cuban expatriates, and God opened incredible doors for me to preach in many churches and in some local secular radio stations. One time I was invited to be the guest speaker on the largest radio station at that time. It was a courtesy interview in honor of my father, as he is considered one of the many martyrs of our country. The gentleman in charge of my interview had heard about my testimony and how I was able, by God's grace, to forgive the people involved in my father's death--including Castro. The radio host told me before the interview that he was totally opposed to my viewpoint. I knew this was not going to be an easy interview.

We started live on the radio, I was able to share how Jesus had healed my heart, and he also asked questions about my dad, and about me personally. Then he stopped and looked at me right in the face and told me, "Lady, do you realize that this is the most powerful station in Miami, and that these radio waves are going throughout all Cuba as well? I responded, "Congratulations!" He proceeded, "I want you to know that the man that was instrumental for your father's murder along with the execution squad and the communist party are hearing you as you speak. What are you going to tell them now that you are talking to them?"

At that moment the room disappeared, and all I could feel was the love of God. I heard myself say, "I have forgiven you. Please forgive yourself, accept Jesus' love, and receive His forgiveness." As I looked up, the radio host had tears in his eyes. He too, was able to forgive! His love also seemed to extend to everyone else in the studio.

And when I went out of the building, a crowd wanting to forgive and to be restored surrounded me. As I look back to this event, I have often wondered whether or not the man who betrayed my father to the Cuban secret police really heard me. Then I think about God's greatness, and I believe that He arranged that meeting as an answer to my prayers for this man.

I continued pastoring my church, occasionally traveling to Miami to share God's love with my fellow countrymen. I saw God do amazing things. I remember one time praying for a man who was covered with terrible skin infections. His arms, his face, and every other visible surface were covered with horrible looking lesions, and he came to the front of the church to receive the prayer of faith. The next day he showed up with brand new skin; it was beautiful, and he was radiant! I remember another man who was dying of cancer, and God healed him instantly. He came back months later saying that all the tests showed that he was cancer free, and now he was going to study to go into the ministry. I remember a young lady that was crippled, and as I prayed and held on to her, her legs became strong, and she was able to walk. Another time God took me to a large Baptist church, and the pastor wanted me to preach regarding the baptism of the Holy Spirit. When I gave the invitation, hundreds of people came forward. I had never seen anything like it, so I did not know what to do, and I heard the Lord saying to me, "Don't worry! You are not doing it anyway. Just pray a mass prayer, and I will take care of it." And He did! It must have been similar to what the day of Pentecost must have looked like! They were all filled with the Holy Spirit. I was so excited! I loved watching God in action! I have many wonderful memories of great miracles, but above all I remember the broken people that were able to forgive those who had done unspeakable wrong to them.

As time went on, it seemed like every time that I would pray, it was not just for Cuba alone. I would have the burden of nations on my heart, and this burden continued to multiply. I could see men, women, and children desperately looking for Jesus, but they could not find Him. I could see Jesus looking for them. I was undone! This went on for years and years and years. I continued to serve as a pastor and evangelist, traveling to Florida and Puerto Rico to reach the Cuban people with the Gospel, and on the way back from one of those trips the Lord said to me, "You will carry my message on television throughout Latin America." I loved that idea, although I scarcely could imagine how it would come to pass.

And then the seed fell to the ground, and it looked like it had died. My work as pastor of the church came to an end. I was to leave the flock and look for lost sheep. But where?

I realized that I had become an evangelist, yearning for "that one lost sheep." The years went by. It seemed like sheep were not so abundant where I was looking. I missed my old congregation terribly, but I continued to cast my net through radio programs, sending the message everywhere an opportunity could be found, preaching at any place I could, but where were the multitude of sheep that I so wanted to tell how Jesus loved them?

And I would remember that the Lord said I would be on television reaching many for Him, and I would go all throughout Latin America telling people how much He loved them. Or did I hear wrong?

Doors opened at a state penitentiary, where I certainly had a "captive audience." These were tough guys. And Jesus showed up again, doing the same thing He does so well, restoring people, healing them and saving them. A man who had been healed of deafness was running the sound for me, and I will never forget my one-armed guitar player! It was quite incredible. I had a lot of fun watching Jesus put together broken lives just like He did mine. In a short time, a church was birthed inside a tough prison setting. I was allowed to baptize them. We ordained deacons, and the warden gave the men a "faith pod" in which they could live and worship virtually free from guards. Many of the men received incredible pardons. Some went on to Bible school and were called into the ministry. Then I heard the Lord saying that it was time to leave this work for another type of ministry. Thus, after two years I said goodbye to the tough guys that became my brothers, and I went looking for more sheep.

One day, one of my brothers in Christ called and said that a local pastor wanted to turn His church over to me. Wow! More sheep! Where? I arrived at the church and met the pastor. He was very discouraged because many of his people had left. The Lord told me, "This is his congregation, I want you to help him build this church." So, I worked with him, helping him with prayer meetings. Jesus honored this commitment in a remarkable way by saving people, healing them, and--doing what Jesus does best--loving them. The church grew, and again it was time to go and look for more sheep somewhere else.

In the meantime the doors opened to go to Latin America to preach, and the Lord brought wonderful results. Many would come to Christ. Many would be healed. I saw so many miracles! There is one in particular that I can never forget. There was a young woman who came to the church were I was preaching. She was about eight months pregnant, and she said that the baby would not move within her womb. She wanted the baby to move, as it should. I prayed briefly for her, for her baby to move, and just as she was leaving, I noticed her feet were very dark--almost black, but by that time, I was not able to reach her; she was gone.

That night I could not stop thinking about her, and I asked the Lord to bring her back so I could pray for her. I was concerned that she could have some kind of blood poisoning, and I feared that the baby was not moving because it might have died in her womb. The next day, she was back in the prayer line, and she again requested prayer. This time I was ready! I asked my friends to help me pray. I rebuked the spirit of death, commanded life to come into the baby, and prayed for total restoration of both the mother and child. Within a few minutes of prayer, the baby started to kick! You should have seen our joy! We were all leaping and praising God for this baby's life. The next day she showed up again in the prayer line, and when I saw her, I was afraid that something had happened, but she only wanted to hug me and tell me that the baby was moving in her womb normally. Her legs were clear. She told me that if the baby was a girl, she would name her Cary, after me! Joy unspeakable and full of glory is what we have when we serve the Lord!

I remember an occasion when I went to preach
in a tiny church in a small town in Oklahoma.
The Lord gave me a Word of Knowledge for a
lady that was sitting in the congregation, and
I told her that God was going to give her the
miracle for which she had asked. I continued
to minister to people, and after a short time, a
young man came to the front. He was on drugs
and could hardly stand up or even open his eyes.
He came to the front and asked for prayer along
with his girlfriend. I could see his pain; the
total captive of a horrible drug addiction, and
my heart went out to him. I said, "Son, call on
Jesus. He will set you free." I asked the church to
help me pray. And all of the sudden, I saw the
young man trying to stabilize himself, screaming
with a loud voice, "Jesus, help me!" The next
thing I heard was this young man speaking out
loud in a most beautiful tongue, worshipping
God totally sober from the drug! Then the lady
to whom I had given the Word of Knowledge
came to the front, screaming at the top of her

lungs, "Thank you, Jesus! Thank you, Jesus!" You see, although I hadn't known it earlier, she was his mother, and God gave her the miracle she was seeking. Her son was free of drugs and came to Christ! Like me, you may have heard that God does not do the same miracles in the United States that He does in other countries, but I clearly do not agree with that statement.

One time when I was in Brazil, I saw an awesome demonstration of God's power. I was in a church of about 250 people north of Sao Paulo. The building was long and narrow, and there was only one entrance to it. The door opened directly into the sanctuary. There was a raised platform in front so people could see the musicians and the preacher. A few stairs had to be mounted to get onto the platform. I was invited to minister, and after I preached, I heard the Lord tell me to have them stand up and pray the following prayer: "Lord, fill us with your power and your fire!"

I did as instructed, and prayed. As I looked
into the audience, I saw the first row of people
appear to be lifted up about two feet into the air.
Each person did a circle in the air and dropped
to the floor. The plastic chairs that were behind
them were pushed back, and then the next row
of people did the same. The next row did the
same and so on until it reached the door at the
back of the room, which was the entrance to the
church! All you could hear was the sound of the
chairs moving on the floor as people were going
under the power of God. The whole church had
been slain in the Spirit! I did not know what to
do. I looked toward the pastor, and he did not
know what to do either. So the pastor, the musicians,
and I continued worshipping God as we saw
all these people fall under the presence of God.
They were crying; they were being filled with the
Spirit; many were going through deliverance,
and others were being healed! And we just kept
on watching!

After ten to fifteen minutes, the congregation
got up, almost in one group movement, and
suddenly they all ran towards the platform
crying, "From now on, we will serve the Lord,
and we will win our city for Christ!" It was
an incredible night. Some threw away their
crutches. People testified of deliverance. Others
dedicated their lives to God. Many received
the Baptism of the Holy Spirit, and Jesus did it
all! No one had laid hands on anyone. It was a
sovereign move of God!

Another time when I was preaching in a small
town near Tulsa, a man came to me for prayer.
The Lord gave him a Word of Knowledge that
he needed to forgive a man who had stolen from
him, and then he would be healed. This man was
suffering from almost uncontrollable diabetes, and
that night he forgave the man who had wronged
him so. God healed him completely. The next
day he came to church telling the people that he
was insulin free, and that God had done the work.

Then he told us the story of how this man had robbed him and his family of their farm; he had hated him ever since, but once he forgave this crime against him, he was healed. During that same revival, a young girl came in and said she could hardly see and wanted her eyes healed. We prayed, and the girl went under the power of God. They had to carry her home like that, but the next day when the girl woke up, her eyes were completely healed. I love to see Jesus in action!

One day, while I was ministering in Mexico there was a young girl about fourteen years old wanting to receive Christ, but she could not say it! Every time she got to the point of speaking those words, she would start moving her head right and left, clenching her teeth, totally unable to speak! We realized that the girl needed deliverance. After prayer she was able to receive the Lord and was filled with the Holy Spirit. She told us her story. She had been involved in witchcraft and was selected by the coven as the new "bride of Satan". They had permanently tattooed her arm indicating so. The girl pulled her sleeve and showed us her arm. We gasped because it was so hideous, but we were thrilled about her salvation. The next day she came into the church, and showed us her arm. Her tattoo had completely disappeared!

During that time I saw another almost blind lady receive her eyesight. I had visited a church in Tulsa and saw this young woman passing me. I had a Word of Knowledge for her and told her that God was going to heal her eyesight. She thanked me and left. The next night we were both at the church. I was able to pray with her, and she instantly received her eyesight.

Another time when I was in Mexico, my good friend Rosario wanted me to come to her mother's home. One of her sisters had learned that she had a tumor in her breast. We prayed for her, and it disappeared! Another sister had trouble with her back, and immediately after prayer we heard bones cracking, and her back was healed. One of her nieces could not chew because her jaw hurt so much. We prayed, and we heard again the cracking of bones--her jaw was healed! There were many more miracles that took place during that visit.

One totally wonderful miracle came to a lady who was about 80 years old. I was ministering and had a Word of Knowledge that she had a bad heart. She confirmed it, and she told me that she was taking medicine for it. We prayed, and she was healed instantly. She went to her doctor who confirmed her healing. A couple of months later she announced that since she was now healed of the heart condition, she was going to get married! And she did.

But then it was time to come home, and I soon was following the same routine. I would work to save money to go back to the mission field and do God's work again. I had always held a secular job while pastoring, evangelizing, and doing the missionary work.

The years kept rolling, and I found that I was far from reaching the multitude of sheep that I had felt was God's promise for me. My heart was broken, and I felt very unfulfilled. It seemed all I could do was pray for the many lost in the world while occasionally doing my trips overseas. It was a really hard time for me, because when I would preach whether in Tulsa or overseas, I would see God doing great things, miracles of all kinds, and above everything, the greatest miracle of all, souls coming to Christ. But then at home, I would hardly get any opportunities to preach or minister. I felt so terribly frustrated.

During that time I started my own business, and God blessed it greatly. This business allowed me to go overseas more frequently, and I was much better able to support my trips. I went on the radio, bought time on local and international radio stations, and continued working to bring many to God. But I questioned myself, and I wondered if that would be the plan for the rest of my life? If that was so, then why was I not completely satisfied? What was missing? Why was I feeling that there should have been more?

I remember during that time reading a story about vessels in the Bible [II Timothy 2:20] and how there are many kinds of vessels. Some are used for drinking water, others for cleansing, still others for ceremonial purposes, and so forth, but there is one that is called the "vessel of honor." This particular vessel is created and then taken to the back of the Potter's shop and left there for years after years until the many colors would appear in the dried clay. The vessel would gather much dust, and it would look very unappealing, but when it was the right time, the potter would bring it out, dust it and the beautiful colors in the vessel would shine again. As I reflected on this

49

particular vessel, I wondered if I was one of those vessels and my beloved Potter had taken me to the back of His shop and forgotten about me...

CHAPTER 3

A SEED
IS SPROUTING

A friend of mine preaches a wonderful message
regarding seeds. He says that when you plant a
seed it goes into the soil looking like a seed.
In the dormant stages the seed breaks the outer
shell, and with a supernatural strength it emerges
through the dirt with a completely different
appearance from when it was planted. In the
process of sprouting, the seed has shed the outer
shell that held it, has developed a root system,

has acquired incredible strength to push the dirt above it, and has brought forth a shoot that will later become a plant that in its maturity will produce a fruit or flower. The fruit or flowers will then have a lot of seeds that eventually will germinate again. They will bring another crop, and then another crop. It will be a never-ending cycle. As long as the seed is willing to die, then the cycle will repeat itself again and again.

This is a great analogy to our lives in Christ. When He plants a dream in our lives, He plants it in seed form. As sad as it might first appear to be, the seed goes into darkness, and in that darkness, it develops the necessary quality, character, and fortitude to mature. Then the Spirit of God infuses the seed He has planted with His strength to push out all things that are in our way in order for the dream to come into fullness and bring forth fruit in due season. Many do not understand this process, and when their seed goes dormant, they give up their dream, thinking it had died. I was one of those, but one day, up from the grave it arose!!!!!

I had been at an evangelistic crusade in Mexico. It was wonderful! Many had come to the Lord. I was interviewed on the radio. The church was packed every night. Jesus was doing miracles right and left. It was awesome! We even had time to visit the local city garbage dump and pray for the people living there. Then it was time to come home. With tears, I left the wonderful people that had labored alongside me as we all worked to bring God's love to so many others.

At home it was business as usual. I had to work overtime for several days to make up for the time I was gone. Busy, busy, busy! And then, I heard God whisper again! "It is time to be on television." And I laughed, just like Sarah in the Bible did when she heard the voice of God saying that she would have a child in her old age! I thought to myself, "You picked a fine time to tell me this. I have no financial support and no church affiliation to carry the huge cost of being on television." Last but not least, I thought, "I don't have any idea of how to do this." There is something about hearing His voice that just cannot be denied. God can have anything He wants! His love compels me. So I said yes. Did I think He had better candidates for this job? Of course I did, and I told Him so. I could think of a million reasons why He could go somewhere else, but I certainly could not escape the one main reason why I was so happy about it: I wanted to tell others how wonderful He is!

So, I started to seek God and to ask Him how He wanted me to accomplish the goal of a television ministry. I knew He had a plan, and I knew that He would show me how to do it. So, little by little, just like holding a rose bud in your hand, and watching it open, the vision started to unfold.

I knew that I must have His exact plans to carry out the work, so I waited for God to tell me. I would pray for specifics. I knew there were many choices, but I wanted to do exactly what He wanted me to do. One day I had a vision and saw two men arguing. One of them wanted to kill himself, and the other one was telling him not to do it. The second man said that once upon a time he himself had wanted to do that same thing, but instead he had surrendered his life to Jesus. Then in my vision I saw myself on television, and I was telling the audience, "Jesus is the same yesterday, today and forever. What He did for this man, He wants to do for you."

So, there it was, the full scope of the work on television that He wanted me to carry out. Because of this vision I realized that I was to do some kind of drama on television and finish it with the presentation of the Gospel and a call for salvation. There were still many questions: is it going to be an hour long, 30 minutes long, weekly, one time? And as I continued to reach out for His instructions, I heard Him tell me,

"You know, Pepsi sells a lot of Pepsi in 30 seconds." So I understood. He wanted me to do "commercials" for Christ.

I was going to need some help regarding actors and production. The instructions I received included producing the best quality programming possible--just like the big television networks. While such a step might seem impossible, all I could think about was that at the other side of the television screen there are many souls, many men, women, young people, old people looking for Him!!!! My earlier vision of LOST SHEEP came forcefully to my mind!!!

As I look back, I realize that He gave me specific crucial instructions on how to get the job done. I did not know the fullness of what was going to take place. My job was to seek Him, to get His instructions, and to obey them one step at the time. Please understand that He only showed me a little bit at a time. I am thankful for this, for if I had known what was ahead, I would likely have been paralyzed with fear. All I knew was that it was going to be a sort of "commercial," of the best quality, and that we were going to be on the largest television stations in Latin America, which, of course, takes lots of money. How much money--I did not even have a clue! I asked God the question as to how this was all to be financed. His response was, "Use your spiritual authority and your faith to bring it about!"

Well, if that was the secret key that I would need, then I would show myself to be diligent in this matter. I bought every book I could get my hands on regarding authority and faith. I read night and day. I would pray and ask God to give me revelation on this subject so that I could use this key to bring about the 90 second spots I had come to envision. I was seriously studying both subjects, knowing that His Word always brings forth the result that He intends to bring forth in a person's heart. I purposely "ingested" all the material related to authority and faith, and to tell you the truth, to this date I have not stopped. I buy all that I can get my hands regarding these subjects because I know that God told me what the outcome would be! Perhaps you are reading this and asking yourself, "What does it mean to use your authority and your faith?" God has delegated His authority to us, His children, to release the things we need in order to bring His will to come to Earth. We are to use our faith to "call those things that are not as though they are," and so I did. As you remember, Jesus taught us to pray, "Thy Kingdom come, Thy will be done on earth as it is in Heaven." I could see that my assignment was to cooperate with God, co-labor with Him, declaring and believing that all the things necessary to do this project would come into my hand. I also filled my heart with specific Scriptures that contained promises regarding bringing to pass the impossible. Prayer, worship, meditation, and intercession became a steady diet in my spiritual life. Then I heard one of my favorite faith teachers saying that if what you want is what God wants, then you will have it. God and I were a team on this.

During the months that followed after I received the word of the Lord regarding the television broadcasts, I noticed a change inside. I was no longer unfulfilled in my longing to reach the lost. I knew that God would make a way to reach that entire multitude that I had seen during my prayer times. I was busy preparing myself for whatever God had ahead for me to do. I knew my little seed was sprouting, and I was going to need His strength to push that dirt off and let the little sprout come forth. It was time to get ready to tell the world that He loves them!!!

I continued to work in my business, continued producing radio programs, and continued doing the missionary work. However, now it was different. We were in sprouting mode…

On a Monday night in December 2004, I went to our weekly prayer meeting and told my friends that I needed help because God had spoken to me. I told them that I had prayed as much as I could, but I was stuck. I needed reinforcement. A beautiful thing took place. No one questioned the vision. Everyone was in one accord that it should come to pass, and the spirit of faith fell upon us. As we started to ask, we believed and received the beautiful dream into reality. It was the first time that I had publicly declared what God wanted to do, and it was accepted by my friends with great joy and anticipation. One of my prayer requests was that I would have the right person to produce the programs--with like heart and calling. We made a list of everything I would need, and each person prayed for the specific item on that list. It was a night filled with faith and anticipation of fulfilling God's greatest mission: the desire to add sons and daughters to His fold!

The next day I contacted Ruben Bonilla, a television producer from Lima, Peru. I had had his e-mail address for quite some time, but after the prayer I felt I had the release to contact him. I wrote to him and asked him if he would be interested in doing commercials for me. I had done some research, and I sincerely believed that a 90 second broadcast was the minimum time necessary to introduce someone to Jesus!

Ruben e-mailed me back the following day saying he was interested in the project, but he was out of the country. This raised my curiosity, and I e-mailed him back asking where he was. The following day he responded that he was in Kansas City, Missouri, about six hours drive from my home. I thought, "Wow! Had the Lord brought him this close?" Yes, He did! So the next day I arranged to meet with Ruben to tell him about my dream and to see if he would be the man this project needed. My girlfriend Jeanne and I arrived at a local restaurant

in Kansas City to meet this soft-spoken young
man. As we had dinner, I told him about
my dream to reach the lost. I told him that I
needed the best quality work because we would
go on the largest television stations. He was
so touched by my dream! Since he was a very
young man, he knew that God would use him
to reach millions for Christ with his producing
ability, and he was waiting for the evangelist
that God would send him.

We all rejoiced and cried with happiness thinking
about all the people that we would reach.

Then he asked how I was going to finance the
project, and I told him that I did not have the
funds to do it, but that God would make a way.

He invited me to go to his home in Lima, Peru,
and stay with his family while we did a pilot of the
program so I would be able to show it to people
with the hope of obtaining funds. Looking

back, I realized that I never questioned Ruben's ability to produce the programs; neither did he question my lack of funds. We both knew that we were doing what we were supposed to do.

So, one month later, I went to Peru. Suddenly I was working with a man whom I had only known for two hours. I was attempting to do a television pilot with no earthly idea of how it was to be done, but I knew that it would allow me to touch many broken hearted people and bring God's love to them.

Yes indeed, we were in sprouting mode!

A Seed Is Sprouting

THIS DIRT IS REALLY HEAVY

We made the television pilot; it was a little harder than I thought it would be. We did it at Ruben's house. It was hot, and it required lots of concentration. It was tremendously hard work in what was to me the very unfamiliar territory of television production. Ruben's family was all wonderful to me. His wife reminded me of my oldest daughter, and in the short time that I was there; I came to love Betty and her gentle personality. Their children were great. All of them were teenagers at that time, and they all worked with their dad. It was a great team effort, and I was proud of being part of the Bonilla team. They had a fun time trying to teach me to be in front of the camera and tell the world that Jesus loves them. I have fond memories of those days, and especially of all of Ruben's wonderful friends and family.

Returning to the USA with the dream made into a pilot, I showed it to my friends, and they loved it. Now I knew exactly how much the cost of the production was going to be, and I thought that once other ministers would see it, I would have an open door in all major ministries--that they would love to pour thousands of dollars into reaching the lost by means of my programs. However, I was wrong. I knocked at many doors, but nothing opened. I was desperate; everyone thought it was great, but not great enough to invest in it. Where was the money going to come from to actually put the programs on the air? Door after door, nothing opened. I tried everything I could think of, but I had no success. At that time the Lord spoke to my heart and said, "Do you want to do this man's way or my way?" That was a bit of a loaded question for me; of course I wanted to do it His way...

Shortly afterward I showed the pilot to some friends. They suggested that I should let them sell the project to a major television network that would carry on the whole vision. This station had the money and it would be done in a professional way. I went before the Lord all excited thinking that this would be the answer, but the Lord said to me that this project was not for sale. So, I declined the offer and I was left wondering which way would the money come in. I kept wondering, what is God's way?

Meanwhile, I kept praying. I was not going to give up. Too many souls were at stake. I was going to co-labor with God for this. Meanwhile, the Lord brought back to my memory the City Dump in Nogales, Mexico, a place where hundreds of people lived in the worst imaginable conditions. Most of the residents are children, single mothers, the elderly, and drug users. It is a really sad place. As I mentioned before, I continued to work in my business and to travel as a missionary/evangelist. My heart was constantly pierced when I remembered the little dirty faces, the hungry people, and the oppressive heat. I had visited in the summer, and there was no water in the area. I remember the elderly suffering under those conditions, and one time I even saw some of the children chasing a snake, because it would be a meal for the family! You have no idea what poverty is like in Latin America! Then I heard God whisper again, "What are you going to do about them?" My human negative reaction was to complain to the Lord, "You have me involved in TV using all my faith to believe for that project, and now you expect me to divert my efforts from the assignment you already gave me! But I could not forget their faces or their need, so I moved ahead, figuring I would have the grace to believe both for the television ministry as well as for the people of Nogales. Somehow God would help improve their lives. But, how?

One day I was asked to share my vision at a local luncheon meeting. I went with my pilot program and showed it to the folks that had come. Everyone loved it and said the same thing, "Go for it sister!" They provided no financial help, but at least they gave me some encouragement. In the crowd was a man named Jerry Morris, and he told me about his work in Latin America. He told me of great acts of kindness that his ministry does for hurting people in Latin countries. He was also involved in developing Christian Schools in local churches, and assisting young kids to receive college education. But the most touching to me were the many children and

adults for whom he has provided medical
assistance by bringing them to Tulsa to have
much needed surgeries, prosthesis, etc. I asked
him if he would consider helping the people
of the Nogales dump. I had contacted other
ministries to see if they would consider digging a
well at the dump, but I was turned down. Those
people needed water so desperately. This gentleman
said that at the moment he could not help
either. A couple of months went by, and it was
his turn to be the guest speaker at the same
local luncheon meeting. I went to hear him,
and again I talked to him regarding help with
the Nogales dump. Again he told me that he did
not think he could help.

A few weeks went by, and I continued to pray
for the people at the dump. Jerry called me to
tell me he was helping a young lady from Cuba
settle in Tulsa, and he wanted me to come to
meet her at his home. It was November, and it
was cold. At Jerry's house I met Nora, a lovely

young woman. She told me about her life in Cuba and how God supernaturally had brought her to Tulsa and to Jerry's house. She was pregnant, her husband had abandoned her, and she reminded me of myself years back. Jerry and his wife Terry had decided to help her by keeping her at their home, taking her to school, and being there for her as she went through her pregnancy. I knew she was in great hands with Jerry and Terry. God had given Nora a spiritual family, and they would be powerful allies for her through whatever struggles she would face.

While we were visiting, I reminded Jerry about the people in Nogales—living on a dusty, dirty, stinky mountain of trash at the City Dump. I think I had to hide some tears from him because I knew that winter was already upon them, and many would not be alive to see spring. They were living in houses made mostly of cardboard boxes, with no running water, no food, and no good winter coats. Winter gets bitterly cold in

Nogales. The temperature can drop below zero, and it also snows occasionally. My visit at Jerry's house was over, and I hugged them and left. As I was driving home, I thanked God for bringing Nora to Tulsa. I prayed that the same grace that was poured on me when I came to Tulsa would also be poured on her. I prayed that a complete restoration would take place in her life.

A day later I received a phone call. It was Jerry. He said to me, "OK, I am on my way to Nogales, Mexico. Give me the name of the local pastor who can take me to your dump." Well, it looked like now I owned a dump! What a sudden promotion in the Kingdom of God! It just so happened that after I left, God spoke to Jerry, and he immediately obeyed. A day later he was flying to observe what I had told him about, and two or three days later he was back to Tulsa. He called me and told me that I was right. He wanted to meet with me urgently. He told me if we did not provide coats, blankets, and food,

some of the people would perish. He had a plan
to obtain donations of all of the above, and he
would get a trailer, drive to Nogales, clear
customs somehow, and take the donated
materials to the people at the dump. He organized
a group to travel with him and we worked very
hard to obtain the blankets, the coats, and the
shoes. It was exciting to see God move for those
people in such a sad, forsaken place in the world.
In less than three weeks everything was ready
to go, and Jerry and his team left for Nogales.
It was going to be the greatest Christmas
possible—both for the team and for the people
living at the dump! All the goods were distributed,
and the Gospel was preached in Word and deed.
Many came to Christ as a result of this effort.

Meanwhile, I continued with my television assignment.
I prayed, fasted, studied, meditated, and asked
others to pray with me, but nothing happened.
At the end of the following year I was totally
exhausted. I had tried every way I knew to raise

funds, and I told the Lord, "I cannot go any farther. I am exhausted. Please fulfill this vision or take this burden from me." I felt I had done a poor job in bringing this vision to pass, and I was ashamed before God. It looked like I was going down in defeat.

Another winter was setting in, and my heart was once more hurting for the people living at the dump. Again we organized a collection of necessary items. Jerry went back and delivered food, toys, and coats. We continued to pray for them. I thought about purchasing a truck that would allow us to carry food daily to them from local churches, but I lacked the funds and the help to bring it about. God would have to do something for these people, but I did not know what.

At the very end of that year Ruben told me, "You have to start producing. We cannot wait any longer, souls are at stake". But I had not been able to raise funds for production costs.

However, I was due a large commission from my business that would pay for one-third of the project, and so I told him, "Let's do it. I will manage to pay for the rest somehow." I commissioned him to start to work on the project. Ruben made plans to be in Tulsa about thirty days later to tape my portion, and at that time he would need to collect the remaining two-thirds of the funds.

Then miracles started to happen. The first leaves had started to appear on the plant growing from my tiny seed. Within the next thirty days I received unexpected commission checks that paid for the rest of the production. Ruben came to Tulsa, and we did our first ten programs. After taping, I felt that all the breath was gone from me, but I was happy when I paid for the programs. I thought that we were ready to go on television, but I was wrong. The program was to be called Minuto Final (which means Final Minute), and I would need to create a trademark and hire a lawyer to copyright the programs. Also, I needed to write a book (containing the plan of salvation) and print it so that I could give it the to viewers who responded to the program. I also needed to produce a media kit to demonstrate to potential partners what the vision was all about. And a website, and copies of DVDs as samples and on and on. As I said goodbye to Ruben, I realized that I needed thousands of dollars more in order to bring about this next phase of the project.

So, back to prayer I went. "God, I need more money! Where am I going to get more money?" He said, "You don't need the money. I am the one who needs it, and when I needed a donkey I called for it." I realized that He wanted this more than I did, and He would take care of it.

With a new found faith and boldness I went around more or less acting as His assistant manager, and I proceeded to arrange for services that were needed to make the program a reality. I knew in my heart that the funds would come in. As I did this, more unexpected commission checks started to appear. One after the other they came, and they were always the right amount every time necessary in order to make the next payment when it that was due. I felt like the widow that had the jar of oil that would not run out. I loved it! I learned what it was like to be in partnership with God! I had found out what is was to do it God's way! I want to explain to you that the checks that came in were above the normal amount of income that my business generated, and I knew that this was God's funding for the programs. I purposed to be a good steward over what God had provided. At first, when the funds started to come, I wanted to use part of it to help the people of Nogales and other struggling ministries. But being a good steward is investing God's money where He tells you. Obedience is the key element in our relationship with God, and it is the only way to find miracles as well.

During the months that followed, I wrote the book, created the media kit, developed the website, and taped my testimony. Ruben prepared multiple DVDs of the testimony, and we shot the first ten programs, three of which he dubbed in English. We worked night and day on this project.

At about the same time a minister I had met asked for a copy of the material to show in Oregon at a convention he planned to attend. He would try to obtain funds for the project. He told me that he needed to have the materials by the following Monday. It was already Wednesday, and Ruben still had the DVDs in Peru. It was impossible to get them to Tulsa by express mail in that short of a time. The only way would be to hand carry them by air. I called a friend of mine who was a missionary in Lima at the time, and I asked him if he knew of anyone coming to Tulsa who could bring me the DVDs. I told him I needed them in Tulsa on Friday. He said he did not know anyone who would be coming the following day.

However, the very next day he called from Peru and told me, "Cary, an amazing thing has happened. Two missionaries from Tulsa were here in Peru, and they were very unfortunately assaulted last night. Because of that, they had to leave for Tulsa today. I was able to ask them if they would take your DVDs, and they said they would. They have your phone number and they will call you when they arrive at Tulsa on Friday with your DVDs!" This was an incredible way for God to answer my prayer! Then I asked my friend for their names and flight information, but he said he had failed to ask. I wondered how I would ever get the materials from them in time to forward them to Oregon.

The next morning I woke up and asked the Lord what to do, but there was no answer. About one o'clock in the afternoon I sensed a prompting in my spirit to go to the airport. I wondered what I would do at the airport since I did not know the people or their specific flight. Nevertheless, I went to the airport. At the luggage retrieval area I saw a large group of people coming from a flight, and I waited there, but I heard nothing. Another large group of people arrived, and again I heard nothing! Yet another group of people came, but still nothing. I thought to myself, I must have missed God in a big way this time! But just then another group of people arrived, and near the back of the crowd I saw a middle-aged lady looking for her luggage. Somehow I just knew that she was the one! I went over to her and said, 'Hello. My name is Cary. Did you by any chance bring my set of DVDs from Lima?" She looked at me as if she had seen a ghost, and she asked, "How did you know I was the one who brought them?" I just smiled. She gave me the DVDs, and I sent one of them to the minister in Oregon. He received it on time and took it to his convention, but

ultimately there appeared to be no positive
result from his efforts.

As I mentioned earlier, I felt we needed to be
able to send a book to people who responded to
the broadcasts. The book would explain the plan
of salvation to people who had no traditional
teaching about being saved. Ruben had helped
me get the book printed in Peru, and we had
saved considerably on the cost of the 10,000
copies we felt we would ultimately need. Now
we needed all those books in Tulsa for distribution,
and as I looked into shipping them to Tulsa, it
was going to be quite an expense. So again I
turned to Jerry Morris. Jerry travels frequently
to Peru, and he graciously agreed to help me
by bringing a suitcase filled with books back
on each trip he made. It is really incredible
that Jerry, his missionary friends, Ruben, and I
brought home all the 10,000 books--one suitcase
at a time with Jerry being the largest contributor
to this portion of our project. What is really

funny is that every time that Jerry would go to Peru, I would ask him to take a partial payment to Ruben, so he would meet Ruben at a Lima's fastfood restaurant and hand him an envelope containing cash. Ruben would give him a suitcase full of books, a practice that might have looked to some as though they were doing a drug deal. Jerry kept saying, "I hope that they don't arrest me for this…" It has been a big joke among our friends ever since; maybe we need to change his name to "God's Smuggler."

Finally, the day came when we were ready to test our first programs. God had told me that we were to be in the largest secular television stations, and so I called one of the largest and requested a quote on their international feed for four 90 second spots five days a week during prime time. I received a quote of $14,000. I called the station for clarification, because I was not sure how many spots could be had for that amount of money. When I spoke with them, they informed me that $14,000 was for only one spot! I was shocked!

I had labored in prayer so long to produce the programs, and now I was not going to be able to pay the money necessary to put them on the air! It seemed impossible that my dream could die such a sudden death! By this time, my faith was so aggressive that I would not give up! God needed these programs to be on the air!

I waited for a few weeks and felt in my heart that I should call the station again and request better rates. I needed boldness, and the thought of the many people waiting to hear about Jesus gave me just exactly what I needed to proceed. I called back, and I explained to them the importance that this type of program carried with it--that people's lives were in the balance. They asked to see the material, and I sent it to them right away. I waited some more, but they did not call, so I called to ask again. At that time

I was informed that they would give me a special rate of $30.00 per spot instead of $14,000, and they said that they would run the spots on prime time four times daily. Yeah!!! God rules!!!!

CHAPTER 5

GUESS WHAT? IT IS AN APPLE SEED!!

The "big day" had arrived. Our pilot program, named "Minuto Final" was about to air. We were able to send the material to a very large television station, and we were ready to bring souls into the Kingdom. I contacted many telephone companies and found out that there was no "1-800-" number available for all of Latin America, so every individual country there would have to have its own telephone number and counseling center. How were all those phone calls going to be answered, and how would I send them the books?

As I pondered on this issue, I had another great surge of boldness. I would call a major ministry that broadcast internationally and ask them to answer the phones and distribute the book. A wonderful lady at the ministry told me that they had never done this, but if I would send them the DVD, they would examine it, pray about it, and let me know. A few weeks went by, and she called me back telling me that they would support my efforts. They were very gracious in all the help they gave us. The broadcast of the program brought an overwhelming response. This ministry answered phone calls, but I personally responded to e-mails sent to me following the program, and I was able to lead many to Christ by that means.

The first spot that we showed had to do with a young lady whose boyfriend was trying to browbeat her into having an abortion. I expected to have a lot a young women writing in, and they did. Several men wrote to me about their plans to commit suicide, and their hearts were turned to Jesus when they saw the spot. I was in shock! I knew God had blessed the spots, and we were going to change the destiny of many people.

Meanwhile, we continued to pray that God would improve the living conditions for the people at the Nogales City Dump. They still lacked water, food, and clothing. One day Jerry called me with great news. He told me that a church wanted to build a mission in the middle of the dump, and he was going to work with the local Mexican pastor to develop this project. Jerry's ministry and his partners purchased the lot. The church purchased the concrete and blocks. Not only did they provide the finances, but also the physical labor. They headed to Nogales and spent a week building the church.

A local Tulsa businessman heard about the project and donated funds to add showers and bathrooms—separate facilities for men and women. Sinks for washing clothes were also donated. Jerry decided to go ahead and build the showers and bathroom facilities but there was no way that we could drill a well on the premises; he was not sure how we were going to get water to this area. So we went back to God, presenting Him with this challenge. Obtaining water at the dump had been a serious issue earlier because there had never been a city water line in the vicinity, but GOD had a way where there seemed to be no other. In the mean time, a nice neighborhood was being planned in another area of Nogales, and in order to provide water for them, the City of Nogales had to place a water line across the dump. It would go right in front of the location where the mission was located. So the City of Nogales became the answer to our prayers for water and bathing facilities for the people at the dump. Jerry was able to connect to local water supply and the people were able to have water!

And there is more. There was now a church on the premises. Jerry, the pastors, and all his wonderful friends connected with other ministries from Tucson, Arizona, and together they worked with the local pastor to provide food, clothing, and medical services on an on-going basis. Also, Jerry would go several times with a medical team. Many have come to Christ through this effort. Their lives are much better. I have been told that the City of Nogales is donating blocks and concrete for them to construct homes, and a local Tucson ministry is providing the manpower. I was so happy for them. God kept teaching me on how to do things His way, which is a lot better than our ways.

Meanwhile Ruben suggested that we participate in COICOM, a trade show for Christian radio and television ministries. I obtained a tiny

booth at their upcoming event and rented a little
TV on which to show our programs. Just as we
were getting ready to go, I heard that very familiar
soft voice telling me something remarkable!
We were to give away all the programs and all
the books rather than sell them to potential
broadcasters. I thought this sounded almost
crazy! How were we going to pay for all this
if we were to give it all away? No, no, no! We
can't do that! There are thousands of dollars
invested, not counting all the hundreds of hours
of work that had been performed! But knowing
that God wanted me to give everything away,
I just obeyed. At the end of the segment the
name and phone number of the ministry, which
had requested to broadcast the program, would
be shown so that people could contact them. I
gave all of these ministries the book that I had
written to accompany the programs, and I even
paid the book's shipping costs. Distributing this
way meant that we would not hear directly from
the people who responded to the programs,

so I would have to trust God that the ministry broadcasting the programs would follow up with the many souls that would be added.

The COICOM convention was in El Salvador that year, and on a hot summer afternoon we arrived, loaded with all the DVDs and media kits to give away. Ruben was there, along with my good friend Rosario, who by then, had become my traveling companion, and one other minister friend, who was in El Salvador preaching at the time. We did not even begin to fit in the booth, as it was so tiny. We started to play the programs. On our first day some broadcasters would stop and listen. Soon I would see a little tear in their eyes, and they would ask me if they could purchase the program for their stations. We would tell them they were free. They were shocked and filled out the application to receive them. On the second day, the word had spread, and people were coming to see the spots. Many requested them for their stations, and others wanted them for use as evangelistic tools. On the third day, the little booth was packed with people asking for the materials. I overheard a comment by one preacher that God had given the Spanish church a new tool to bring in the lost, and that tool was called Minuto Final! At the end of the trade show we left with lots and lots of applications requesting the programs and the books. They were so many I was in shock! Rosario and I began the task of sorting all the names and countries, and all of Latin America was represented. We noted all of the different stations that the program would be on, and I realized that the strategy of giving all the materials away was truly successful. God only needed someone to obey.

Ruben quickly started producing the programs, and in January of 2007 Minuto Final went on the air all over Latin America. It was a dream come true!

Every so often we would get an e-mail thanking us for the program, and sometimes we would get a testimony of salvation. However, there were not many of these because we had been directing people to a local church. This, again, was part of God's strategy. He wanted the believers to be plugged into a local church. Thus, God's plan was much more complete than anything that I might have designed simply by myself.

Meanwhile, we kept producing programs, ten at a time. I would receive an unexpected amount of money, and I would treasure it because I knew it was to be for the production of more programs. At times I would get a little desperate because our progress was so slow, and I was concerned that we would be dropped from individual stations due to having so many reruns. But we were not dropped! God was blessing the work, and many were being added to the kingdom.

One time I received an e-mail from a pastor who told me that he had decided to build a church

in a small country town, and he placed Minuto
Final on the local television station. He said that
the people would call after the program. He
told me he had planted a very thriving church
using Minuto Final as their evangelist. I was
really happy to hear this! Another time I
received an email from a pastor who said that
whenever he gave out our little book, "From
Failure to Success," lost people would start to
tremble and cry, and they would read the book
and come to Christ. Twice more I received
similar e-mails from different countries
requesting "the book that makes people cry and
tremble." I pondered all of these happenings in
my heart, and I decided that God was using this
little book as a sign and wonder.

We attended COICOM a second time and a third
time. At that point we were so well known that
people were waiting at our booth to obtain our
material. We also produced Minuto Final for
radio. I was so happy thinking about all the

people that we were impacting. People were coming to the booth telling us about the results that they were having with Minuto Final.

As time went by and more stations were added, people started to look for Minuto Final on the internet. The e-mails started to grow along with the prayer requests, and one day as I was having lunch with Eric and Amy, more wonderful friends, that saw what God was doing and they said to me, "You must start to nurture and disciple these people through e-mails." Eric volunteered his sizeable expertise on internet applications, and we began using it to teach the many people who wrote to us. I was completely amazed at the number of e-mails received daily. We had begun to minister to a weekly congregation of thousands of people. Most of them came from a Catholic background. We got many prayer requests and frequent praise reports. Our programs are viewed over all Latin America, the USA, Canada, and parts of Europe and Africa. Millions of people are watching them daily.

One of the scriptures that I found to be very important for me on this project is Mathew 24:14: "This gospel shall be preached to all nations, and then the end will come." I believe that Minuto Final is one of the many tools that God is using to fulfill this Scripture. Last year, I felt in my heart that He wanted us to go into the Muslin world and have our programs dubbed into Egyptian Arabic. A few months later, I was connected with an Egyptian brother who saw my material and took an interest in it. Recently, he has told me that we will be able to air the programs on four different satellite stations that beam to all the Islamic people worldwide. They will respond to e-mails, and they have a plan to position the new believers within underground churches. He said that the stations will donate the airtime if I provide the dubbed material. I am asking God for the finances to do this.

After Arabic translation, I believe there will be another language, and another, and another. How many? As many as I can believe Him for. How many apples are in an apple seed? No one knows, but there are many. The seed He planted in my heart is like an apple seed, and it will produce a tree with many apples on it, each one of which can multiply to many more trees, and so forth as God ordains. The same is true for you! Your part is to believe that all things are possible with Him.

The next door that God has opened is the radio. I am currently getting ready to start doing a live daily radio program that will impact another set of listeners. It will be aired throughout the United States and all of Latin America. The title of the radio program will be "Conflicts of the Heart." People will be able to call in and obtain Christian counseling for their problems, and we will educate them in the Word of God and pray for them. I am really excited; it is going to be a great opportunity to tell many about His love. In the last few months, I have also been busy writing. It seems to please the Lord that we use all methods of communication to spread the Gospel. The time is short.

I have neglected to tell you something really important. God gave me the funds to invest into this project. I believed Him for it, and He came through. It did not come the "regular way," but as I told you, at the beginning, God asked me clearly if I wanted to do this by man's way or by His way. I really did not know what He meant by that, but what I do know is that His way is better than ours. He led me down an unusual path, but it was a good path. Many people are sitting on the benches waiting for contacts, money, or some other manifestation of God's power. But it is not until you act that God will show you what can happen.

Another important thing that I learned in this process is that I had to give what was in my hand for God to bless it and multiply it. That is a very important truth. If I had not obeyed the Lord in giving, I would not be telling you this story. As a result of my obedience, I have received all that I needed and more to take care of the needs of the ministry. We have now produced a total of 60 programs in three years. It has been a slow process in the production sense, but I am trusting that we will be able to produce 60 more programs every year from now on! I am praying that God will add prayer warriors and financial partners to this ministry so we can increase our momentum.

At the end of last year, my business suddenly disappeared. I performed export management services for a small number of customers whose businesses I had worked long and hard to develop. It had allowed me to have freedom of time and a good income. But my customers either retired, or they decided to hire a full time employee because I had grown their businesses to that extent. I had operated my business for more than 14 years, but it had come to a close. I was very concerned about this, because God had always provided through my secular work, not only for my needs but for the ministry. However, I felt a release to give my time completely to the work of the Lord, and in doing so, I have stayed very busy indeed! When I first started with Minuto Final, God spoke to my heart that there would be a time when a change in my business operations would take place—at which time He would add partners to help with the work rather than my having to rely solely on my personal finances. So now I am in a new phase with God. It is different! I love it, and I am doing what I am supposed to do--trusting in Him. Walking with God is never boring!

CHAPTER 6

WHAT ABOUT YOUR DREAM?

Your dream is important to God, and it is also important to me because we are both part of the body of Christ. If one part is "sick" or "weak," all the other parts are affected as well. All His parts should be healthy and functioning to the perfection for which they were created.

I want to tell you what God taught me that caused my dream to come to pass.

God has imprinted on our being His vision for our lives, and the sooner we get on to fulfill it, the happier we will be. Your vision starts with your identity and your purpose in life. Your vision, whether it is the ministry, a business, or a career, has your identity built into it, and it will bring God's purpose to fruition in your life and in the lives of many others.

So often people go around with an unfulfilled dream in their lives, and they seem to say, "Well, I am available if God wants to use me." I did that for quite some time, but then I learned better. I learned that God has given us authority to bring the dreams He has put within us to pass, and it is up to us to pursue His daily leading in order to make the dream come to pass. Just as we "pursue" the air we breathe, we need to pursue our dream with all of our being.

God wants you to fulfill the dream He put within you, but the enemy of your soul does not want it. So, a battle will ensue, probably one that has already been ongoing for quite some time, but Jesus has already won that battle at the cross. It is up to you to enforce the enemy's defeat and declare your victory regarding your life and your dreams.

Jesus performed all His miracles, signs, and wonders as one who was in right relationship with God. You, as a born again believer, share that same relationship as a joint-heir with Jesus. God wants you to possess what he says belongs to you!

I believed in my dream, and I had been praying that it come to pass since 1984. That was the year that God burned into my heart the condition of the lost people in Latin America. I have had a prayer burden since then. I believe that all these years have been in preparation for what has only recently appeared to be coming to fruition. And during the first year when the vision was revealed to me, my prayer life intensified as I started to co-labor with God to bring it to pass.

You might ask, what do you mean to "co-labor" with God? It means to come into full agreement with what God wants to do **in** your life and **through** your life in order to bless people. It means to see the work He wants you to accomplish--from His perspective. It means to be totally dependent on the Holy Spirit. When you start to see the work from God's perspective, then you go around saying "God has need of this," and "this" will come in. It means learning to receive power from on high and also learning to release that power to change the opposing circumstances, whatever they might be.

When you co-labor with God, you are His steward on this earth, and you will be able both to command and also to release His will on earth. His Kingdom come; His will be done. It is His will that all men be saved--that none perish. So you release anointed faith-filled words to declare what He has shown you His will is. Some of you that are reading this might be a little surprised by this, but God created the world with His Words, and we are created in His likeness, so just like He does, we must also do. We must create with our words what God wants to be done on earth. We have been given authority to decree, to proclaim, and to bring to pass His will in our lives. If we don't do it, it will not get done. And along with this authority we have been given the faith to bring it in.

A large part of my prayer life has been declaring and commanding a release of favor, finances, key relationships, and wisdom. Another large part of my prayer life has been study and meditation on the Word of God and praying in the Spirit. As God had told me specifically that my authority and faith would bring this dream to pass, I devoured every book available to me regarding authority and faith. I lived and breathed authority and faith. And let me tell you, it has produced results in my life.

I remember when I went to San Pedro Sula, Honduras, to preach. I had been told that we were in the same room that had been used earlier by the Organization of American States, which gathers officials from all the countries of the Western Hemisphere together. We were the very next ones to occupy that location. The amount of security just before I arrived was overwhelming since all the Secretaries of State of the various countries were present. As I was approaching the pulpit to address the meeting, the Lord spoke to my heart and told me that the walls of that building had heard of developed plans that were against His will. He asked me to take care of it. So, when I got to the pulpit, my greeting was: "Good morning. We have some serious work to do." And we proceeded to bring down all the work of the enemy against Honduras and the Latin countries in prayer and declared them free to serve God. What I did not know was that a civil war was about to take place that day. Many feared bloodshed in the streets, and everyone was prepared to go into hiding. Needless to say, it did not happen. We left, and although a week later the country went into some turmoil, God prevailed and rescued the people of Honduras from a communistic coup. As of today, the country of Honduras is still free to serve God.

As a young Christian, God took me to a local church where faith and authority were taught on a regular basis. Great men and women of God--true giants of faith--enriched my life. I learned what it was to walk in authority. As a small example of this, once a plague of armyworms came to my hometown, and it had been said that they would devour all the grass in sight. I had a pretty lawn and was distraught at the idea that it would die. So, when I got back from church, I walked along the property and

declared that none of these worms would come
into my yard and that they would not eat my
grass. The worms did come to my neighborhood,
but my yard was the only one that they did not
eat. As I grew in God, my spiritual authority
grew to more than authority over mere worms.
I took authority over sickness, disease, and other
issues that were very important.

Along with authority, you have to have faith. If
you don't believe what you just declared, you
might as well go home, because nothing will
take place. You must believe! Faith brings you to
a realm where things can only be accomplished
with the power of God.

The opposite of faith is unbelief. One way to get
rid of unbelief is fasting. When God told me we
were going to go on TV, the first thing I did was
a long fast, because I knew that inside I had
unbelief, and I needed to eliminate it. Every
time I need to do something bigger than

normal, I fast. I need all the unbelief removed!
I suggest you try it; it works!

If you have faith, you won't have doubt. You
can't have both; it is one or the other. It is like
having light and having darkness. They don't
dwell together. Faith is better. Faith moves you
to God's side of His world. Faith allows you
to receive without tangible proof. However,
when you have faith, it will manifest in due time.
When? In God's due time. Our flesh does not
want to wait, but we must wait on His timing.
We don't see the whole picture as He does, and
He knows when it is best for the final result to
appear. In the meantime, we must continue
in faith for whatever we are pursuing. Having
faith is like being pregnant; you have conceived,
but no one can tell it for a while. However, you
know it, and one day it will be manifested to all!

You must not neglect corporate prayer. It brings
your petition to a different realm and according

to His Word the unity in corporate prayer will bring greater reinforcement for what you are praying about. God blessed me with many prayer warriors. They have impacted my life with their prayers and faith. They have declared, imparted, activated, or simply given me "a push in the Spirit." This allowed me to reach my goal faster and more easily than I would have, had I been doing it all alone. I am very grateful to each and every one of them for their role in my life. I honor them and love them, and I know that they have labored with me for this work to come to pass.

I remember going to one of our prayer meetings. I stood in the living room at the house of my friend Dee, and I announced we were ready to take off and conquer! And take off we did. All the women rallied around me, and we prayed and believed for the impossible, and it happened. Our prayer times are very precious to me, and I encourage you to have a body of believers with whom you can pray, and not only pray but also share with them what God is saying to you. This can confirm the direction of the Holy Spirit in your life.

Prayer is a lifestyle. You live in constant relationship with Him. You talk to Him, discuss important issues, and tell Him of your dreams. Prayer means pursuing the will of God and coming in agreement with Him. There are times where you labor in prayer until you think you have poured your entire heart out, and you feel that there is no more spiritual energy within you. There are other times when He brings you to levels of authority in the Spirit to decree His Word and release His will. This special relationship is hearing what He wants you to pray, and then doing it exactly as He instructed you. From time to time His instructions for specific situations may change, but the relationship remains the same.

There are certain things that will deter you from obtaining your dream. Satan is our number one enemy, but he is already defeated. He tries to use people to destroy our faith and our purpose in life. He tries to use our innermost thoughts to make us think that we are defeated—that we will never amount to anything. That is a lie from the very pit of Hell itself. The Bible tells us clearly that we exist because of the Cross of Christ, where he purchased our salvation, our healing, our freedom, and our total restoration. After His resurrection, the Holy Spirit took on the work of glorifying the Son, shaping us in His image. As He is, so are we. Therefore, we are seated in Heavenly places with Christ Jesus. We have a place at the throne with Christ. We are God's children and His heirs. He will not withhold anything good from us. And as mature children, it is time we go about taking care of the Father's business.

Ask God to lead you to a good prayer group. As I mentioned before, I was surrounded by

wonderful prayer warriors and friends that loved
me and believed with me for the impossible. But
then, we all have certain friends and family members
that do not understand our vision because their
level of maturity in Christ is just not there. You
must guard your heart when you are around
them. Keep your dreams covered in this case.
Don't let them out where you know that they
will be stepped on. These are the people that the
enemy will use to discourage you and deter you
from your dream. Don't blame them, because
if they knew that they were being used by the
enemy, they would feel really bad. Just love
them and protect your dreams. Don't expose
your dreams to this type of negative influence.

A long time ago I read in a book a statement
that I will always remember. It concerned the
life of Smith Wigglesworth. He said that he
would never say what he was about to do in
public, because when he did, he would have
to fight the devil on that issue. Learn from his

wisdom; keep your dream within your assigned prayer warriors until it comes to pass. Then you can show the Devil that it is too late. You are already on your way!

Many people try to fight the Devil, but he has already lost, so why continue a constant battle with him? Just inform him of his defeat, and he will flee from you. You have a right to all good things that God has delegated to you. Until I received the revelation that He has done it all, I was not able to enforce the spiritual authority that would demand the release of what God had given me. The enemy wants to destroy your faith, because without faith, it is impossible to please God. You have to have faith.

As I mentioned before, you can increase your level of faith through fasting and constant exposure to the Word of God. Most important, you must act on it. If you have faith and don't use it, it is useless. If you have not started practicing your faith, then start small with small things in your everyday life. God will show you that He is blessing these areas, and this will inspire you to start believing for even larger things. The more you practice faith, the easier it will become to have deep, sincere faith for the really big things that everyone has to face from time to time in life. Train yourself to be in communion with God at all times, asking, believing and receiving. It is fun! The subject of faith is very important. God is a faith God. You came to Christ through your faith. You maintain your relationship with Him through faith. You will die in faith. The Bible says that precious in the eyes of the Lord is the death of his saints. I believe that dying is our last act of faith on this earth, as we take a big step of faith right through Heaven's gate. God likes that. He likes for us to trust him. I guess what it all boils down to is having a wonderful relationship with God the Father, God the Son, and God the Holy Spirit. It is the daily walk with Him that allows you to hear, converse, trust, and obey. If you have not made the decision to trust Him with your life, why don't you take time and give your heart to Him right now. It is not saying a few "magic" words. It is bringing your heart to Him in all honesty and saying, "I believe in you. I need you. I love you. Take what I am, and make me yours!

I know that God has something wonderful prepared for your life. I know that you have a dream that you have not fulfilled yet. But this moment—right now!--is the beginning of fulfilling your dream. Start with prayer, talk to God, and ask Him. He wants to answer. Go on a fast. Get rid of your unbelief by moving to God's side. Start seeing the world through His eyes, become His steward, and you will see a great change both within you personally and in your dreams.

All things are possible to him that believes!

Notes

Notes

Notes

Notes

Notes

Notes

Notes

Notes

Notes

Notes

Notes

Notes

Notes

Notes